Creating
Meaningful
Funeral
Ceremonies

A Guide for Caregivers

Alan D. Wolfelt, Ph.D.

Also by Alan Wolfelt, Ph.D.:

A Child's View of Grief

Death and Grief: A Guide for Clergy

Healing the Bereaved Child: A Growth-Oriented Approach to Caregiving

Helping Children Cope with Grief

Interpersonal Skills Training: A Handbook for Funeral Home Staffs

Sarah's Journey

Understanding Grief: Helping Yourself Heal

Companion
P R E S S

Companion Press is dedicated to the education and support of both the bereaved and bereavement caregivers. We believe that those who companion the bereaved by walking with them as they journey in grief have a wondrous opportunity: to help others embrace and grow through grief — and to lead fuller, more deeply-lived lives themselves because of this important work.

Companion Press is a division of The Center for Loss and Life Transition, located in Fort Collins, Colorado.

For ordering information, write or call:

Companion Press
A division of
The Center for Loss and Life Transition
3735 Broken Bow Road
Fort Collins, CO 80526
(303) 226-6050

Creating Meaningful Funeral Ceremonies

A Guide for Caregivers

Alan D. Wolfelt, Ph.D.

Companion Press is an imprint of the Center for Loss and Life Transition,
3735 Broken Bow Road, Fort Collins, Colorado 80526

Manufactured in the United States of America

ISBN: 1-879651-08-4

This resource is dedicated to the participants in the first "Exploring the Principles of Growth-Oriented Grief Counseling" seminar held at the Center for Loss and Life Transition. They encouraged me to explore this material with them. During our week together we laughed, we played, we cried and we participated in a ritual that will bind us together forever.

You are my friends and life companions.

June Benton
Carol E. Blom
Neil de Rijk
Teresa Dutko
Diane Duvall
Mary Ann Gour
Lorraine Gyauch
Susan Hannon
Harold Heidegger
Georgia Huckeby
Ed Jensen
Sr. Diane Liona
Sue Maxymiv
Judith Montelione
Paul Montelione
Jude Ramirez
Dar Richardson
Val Slater
Rob Smith
Bridget Tisthammer

Contents

Preface

"(Ritual) is a pattern imposed on the mere flux of our feelings by reason and will, which renders pleasures less fugitive and griefs more endurable, which hands over to the power of wise custom the task (to which the individual and his moods are so inadequate) of being festive or sober, gay or reverent, when we choose to be, and not at the bidding of chance."

C.S. Lewis

I have had the privilege of "companioning" thousands of bereaved people who have been willing to teach me about their grief journeys. I also have experienced how my own personal losses have changed my life forever. In these ways I have learned that meaningful funeral ceremonies are one of the most affirming means of helping our fellow human beings begin to embrace the pain of separation and loss after the death of someone loved.

Meaningful funeral ceremonies can and do make a significant difference in how the bereaved channel their grief toward health and healing. During the funeral the community comes together and responds not only to the reality that someone has died, but to the reality that those remaining will need support, compassion, love, hope and understanding. More, an authentic funeral is often the beginning of the expression of grief. What happens at the funeral (and how it happens) greatly affects how the bereaved go on to find meaning and purpose in their continued living.

*H*elen Keller provided us with a simple yet profound metaphor when she said, "The only way to get to the other side is to go through the door." Meaningful funerals are doorways to healing for the bereaved.

Helen Keller provided us with a simple yet profound metaphor when she said, "The only way to get to the other side is to go through the door." Meaningful funerals are doorways to healing for the bereaved. Some mourners, following the current North American trend away from funerals, are choosing never to enter the doorway. Many,

Companioning the Bereaved

To "companion" the bereaved means to be an active participant in their healing. When you as a caregiver companion the bereaved, you allow yourself to learn from their unique experiences. You let the bereaved teach you instead of the other way around. You make the commitment to walk with them as they journey through grief.

unaware of the ways in which authentic funerals can help them, are blindly choosing doorways that lead nowhere. But a lucky few are led through the very special doorways that open onto the many paths to grief's reconciliation. You, the bereavement caregiver, have the opportunity to lead mourners through doorways that are best for them.

As a death educator and grief counselor, I am writing *Creating Meaningful Funeral Ceremonies* out of a deep concern that individuals, families and ultimately society as a whole will suffer if we do not reinvest ourselves in the funeral ritual. Helping the bereaved create meaningful funeral ceremonies may be one of the most important things we as caregivers can do. I hope the information in this booklet will challenge you to help create a personalized, meaningful funeral for every bereaved family in your care.

The primary purposes of this booklet are to outline the central influences of the deritualization of funerals in contemporary North America, explore the primary purposes of meaningful funeral rituals, review qualities in caregivers that help make them effective facilitators of meaningful funeral rituals and provide practical ideas to assist in the creation of authentic, personalized and meaningful funeral ceremonies.

"'Tis the good reader that makes the book," said Ralph Waldo Emerson. That observation applies especially to this type of resource. This text, written for people willing to constantly strive to improve their skills in creating and leading authentic funeral rituals, will do little good if its messages are exiled to the reader's mental bookshelves. Instead I challenge you to consider *Creating Meaningful Funeral Ceremonies* each time you plan a new funeral and to persistently and creatively strive to improve your ability to bring meaning to the funeral experiences of those you "walk with" in grief.

My wish for you is that the information and ideas in this booklet will inspire you to the benefit of those you help. As you read *Creating Meaningful Funeral Ceremonies*, I invite you to share your own ideas about funerals with me. Please drop me a note to express your views about this important area of bereavement ministry.

Cordially,

Alan D. Wolfelt, Ph.D.
Director, Center for Loss and Life Transition

Introduction

"Show me the manner in which a nation or a community cares for its dead and I will measure with mathematical exactness the tender mercies of its people, their respect for the law of the land, and their loyalty to high ideals."

William Gladstone

We as a culture appear to be forgetting the importance of the funeral ritual. While funerals have been with us since the beginning of human history, many North Americans are now deciding that funeral rituals don't have a place in their lives. We seem to be rapidly moving toward the dominant Anglo-Saxon model of minimizing, avoiding and denying the need for rituals surrounding death.

The Cremation Association of North America (see charts at right) reports that in 1992, 19.11% of all the people who died in the U.S. were cremated, up from the 1962 figure of 3.61%. The same organization projects the U.S. cremation rate will surpass 35% by the year 2010, and climb even higher beyond that. The Canadian figures mirror and even outpace this trend. (A regional caveat: The use of cremation varies greatly by region. In the U.S., for example, states with 1992 rates higher than 40% included Colorado, Washington, Oregon and Nevada. On the opposite end of the spectrum were West Virginia, Alabama, Mississippi and Kentucky—all with cremation rates less than 4%. In Canada, the 1992 rates for the eastern part of the country were 29.28% (projected to be 42.55% in 2010), whereas the rates for western Canada were 50.71% (projected to be 74.97% in 2010.)

What's troubling about this overall trend toward cremation? Many North Americans who choose cremation also choose not to have an accompanying service, thereby avoiding the funeral ritual altogether. While we do not know what portion of the current 19% receives direct cremation with no funeral service (CANA has recently initiated a study to determine that), my experience with funeral service suggests that many of the growing numbers of North Americans requesting cremation do not partake in an accompanying ritual. (By contrast, 69.24% of all England's 1992 deaths ended in cremation, many with some form of funeral service—certainly a healthier combination.)

Cremation Rates in the United States

1962	3.61%
1972	4.94%
1982	11.73%
1992	19.11%
2010	35% (projected)

Cremation Rates in Canada

1962	3.58%
1972	7.21%
1982	20.26%
1992	35.43%
2010	52.26% (projected)

Source: The Cremation Association of North America

Many would attribute the rise in direct cremation to the high cost of today's traditional funeral. On the contrary, CANA reports that just 18% of the people electing cremation do so because of the lower price tag. So, it would seem, our current aversion to the funeral is motivated less by money and more by the deritualization influences I will put forth in this text.

This is certainly not to say that cremation as a form of disposition is inherently bad; many cultures use cremation together with ceremony to create beautiful funerals. In fact, used creatively and flexibly, cremation can actually increase a bereaved family's ceremony options. And while having the body present at the visitation or funeral can aid the grieving process (see p. 10), there are certainly forms of bodiless ceremonies that make meaningful rituals. Too often, though, we are using cremation without services (and sometimes body burials without services) as a way to circumvent death and avoid the pain of grief.

Creating meaningful ceremonies when death impacts us can assist us with emotional, physical and spiritual transformations. The death of someone we love often temporarily disconnects us from ourselves and the world around us. As we search for some sense of balance, we must make internal adaptations to our new outer reality—someone who has been physically present in our lives is

Most people do not understand why funeral ceremonies help us adapt to change and heal.

gone. Participating in a meaningful funeral ceremony helps us begin to recenter ourselves, to make that painful but necessary transition from life before the death to life after the death. In my work with thousands of bereaved people, however, I have found that most people do not understand why funeral ceremonies help us adapt to change and help us heal (at least not until they have experienced a meaningful funeral service.)

Part 1:
Influences on the Deritualization of the Funeral

For many, traditional funeral rituals have lost much of their value and meaning. They are perceived as empty and lacking creativity. I myself have attended way too many of what I would term generic funerals—cookie cutter ceremonies that leave you feeling like you may as well have been at a stranger's funeral. As more and more people attend these meaningless funerals, society's opinion of the funeral ritual in general nosedives. This in turn causes people to devalue the funeral that will be held for them someday: "When I die, don't go to any trouble." A tendency to minimize one's own funeral is for many a reflection of the sense of purposelessness they have witnessed while attending a generic funeral service.

Let's explore a few of the other causes of the deritualization of the funeral service in North America:

· **We live in the world's first death-free generation.**

Many people now live into their 40s and 50s before they experience a close personal loss. Today two-thirds of all deaths in the U.S. each year happen to people 65 or older. One result of this mortality rate shift is that if you are forty or older and have never attended a truly meaningful funeral, you probably don't realize the importance of having one.

In the early 1900s, on the other hand, most children had been to many funerals by the age of ten. (In 1900 over half of all deaths in the U.S. each year were deaths of children 15 or younger.) Aging, illness and death were an everyday part of family life. While we certainly appreciate the medical advances that have helped lower the mortality rate and prolong lifespans, they are also distancing us from aging, illness, death, grief—and thus the funeral ritual.

· **We live in a mobile, fast-paced culture.**

Tremendous geographical distances often separate family members and friends today. Fifty years ago, friends only had to walk down the street to be a part of a funeral; now it is not unusual for them to fly in from thousands of miles

"To forget one's ancestors is to be a brook without a source, a tree without a root."

Chinese proverb

7

away. This isn't convenient, and we are a convenience-based culture. If it isn't easy, we often just don't do it.

Have you also noticed how we like many things to be fast in our culture? It seems that efficiency or speed is often placed above effectiveness. This often goes hand-in-hand with "cheaper is better." So, some people combine the thought that direct cremation with no services will be fast and cheap. Yet, while this may be true, some survivors may pay an emotional price for years.

· **We value self-reliance.**

Have you noticed that the biggest section in bookstores these days is the self-help section? We live in an era of rugged individualism and independence. We reward people for "doing it on their own." How many of us grew up learning the North American motto, "If you want it done right, do it yourself"? Yet, when someone in your life dies, you must be interdependent and connected to the world around you if you are to heal. In short, rugged individualism and funerals don't mix well.

· **We eschew spiritualism.**

As our society becomes more educated, we seem to be adopting a more academic orientation to life and death. As I travel throughout North America, I observe that some of the largest pocket areas of direct cremation with no ceremony are in highly populated, academic communities. In a 1962 study, sociologist Robert Fulton confirmed that people who doubt the usefulness of funerals are more likely to be highly educated, professionally employed and financially well-off. Observational research of today is consistent with Fulton's 30-year-old findings.

Of course, many among this highly educated population would argue they have found a substitute for the old-fashioned, "morbid" funeral: the memorial service. It seems that the more educated one becomes, the more "at risk" one becomes for not participating in death rituals. The potential problem with memorial services is twofold: 1) they are often delayed until a more convenient time weeks or months after the death, and 2) the body is often not present. These factors tend to encourage mourners to skirt the healing pain that funerals— because of their timeliness, their focus on embracing a variety of feelings, including pain (not just joy), and their use of the body as reality check—set in motion. How many times have you heard someone leave a memorial service

> *How many of us grew up learning the North American motto, "If you want it done right, do it yourself"? Yet, when someone in your life dies, you must be interdependent and connected to the world around you if you are to heal.*

saying, "Wasn't that great! No one even cried!"? While some memorials are certainly meaningful and authentic, I am suggesting that too often they do healthy mourning a disservice.

· **We don't understand the role of pain and suffering.**

Another major influence on the deritualization of death in our culture is our avoidance of pain. We misunderstand the role of suffering. People who openly express their feelings of grief are often told to "carry on", "keep your chin up" or "just keep busy." Worse yet, some bereaved people are greeted with theologized clichés like "God wouldn't give you any more than you can bear," and "Look at it this way . . . now you have an angel in heaven." This misuse of doctrine is used by some for the purpose of suppressing "incorrect" thoughts and feelings.

Shame-based messages like the above examples result in some bereaved people thinking that mourning (i.e. sharing your grief outside yourself) is bad. If you are perceived as "doing well" with your grief, on the other hand, you are considered "strong" and "under control." Of course, it is easier to stay "rational" if you don't participate in a ceremony that is intended to, among other things, encourage you to embrace feelings and acknowledge a painful reality.

· **We have lost the symbolism of death.**

Deritualization also appears to be influenced by a loss of death's symbols. Ariès, in his book *The Hour of Our Death*, identifies the symbols representing death in art and in literature, as well as in funeral and burial customs. He maintains, and I agree, that symbols of death are no longer prominent in contemporary North American culture, and that gone with them is a link that in previous generations provided meaning and a sense of continuity for the living.

In generations past, for example, the bereaved used to wear mourning clothes or armbands, often black, that symbolized their sorrow. In some subcultures, mourners also hung wreaths on the door to let others know that someone loved had died. Today we can't even tell who the bereaved are. For some, memorial flowers, both at the funeral and at the cemetery, are becoming another ousted symbol. Today we opt for the more practical but less spiritual monetary donation: "In lieu of flowers, please send contributions to . . ."

Perhaps the ultimate symbol of death that we are tending

"When a person is born, we rejoice. When they are married, we celebrate. When they die, we pretend nothing happened."

Margaret Mead

9

more and more to forsake is the dead person's body. When viewed at the visitation or during the funeral service itself, the body encourages mourners to confront the reality and the finality of the death. Of course, opponents of viewing often describe it as unseemly, expensive, undignified and unnecessary. Yet, seeing and spending time with the body allows for last goodbyes and visual confirmation that someone loved is indeed dead. In generations past, the body often served as the very locus of mourning; the bereaved came to the dead person's home to view the body, pay their last respects and support the primary mourners. In fact, the body was often displayed for days before burial. Today, with our increasing reliance on closed caskets and direct cremation with no services, we are forgetting the importance of this tradition.

Perhaps the ultimate symbol of death that we are tending more and more to forsake is the dead person's body. When viewed at the visitation or during the funeral service itself, the body encourages mourners to confront the reality and the finality of the death.

As Ariès writes, "The change (in death's role in our society) consists precisely in banishing from the sight of the public not only death but with it, its icon. Relegated to the secret, private space of the home or the anonymity of the hospital, death no longer makes any sign." As we eliminate the symbols of death, we also appear to be eliminating the rituals, historically rich in symbolism, that remind us of the death of others as well as our own mortality.

- **We deny our own mortality.**

One woman said to me recently, "I don't do death." She is not alone. Many people in North America today deny their own mortality and thus the need for rituals surrounding death. In his book *The Funeral: Vestige or Value*, author Paul Irion calls this "assumed invulnerability." He reflects that, "Man knows that he is only assuming invulnerability, that he is ultimately vulnerable, and yet to admit this fact totally is to be defenseless." In other words, denying our own mortality is better than the alternative.

Sigmund Freud also wrote of this theme in his *Collected Papers* when he concluded, "At bottom no one believes in his own death, or to put the same thing in another way, in the unconscious every one of us is convinced of his own immortality."

The increasingly popular belief in cryonics is perhaps the ultimate manifestation of our mortality denial. One of the largest cryonics groups had 353 members in 1993, up from 29 in 1983. Through cryonics, which involves the freezing of a dead body (or sometimes just the head of a dead body) and its

Funeral misconceptions

- *Funerals are too expensive.* The social, psychological and emotional benefits of authentic funerals far outweigh their financial costs. Besides, a funeral needn't be lavishly expensive to be meaningful.

- *Funerals make us too sad.* When someone loved dies, we need to be sad. Funerals provide us with a safe place in which to embrace our pain.

- *Funerals are barbaric.* On the contrary, meaningful funeral ceremonies are civilized, socially binding rituals. Some people think that viewing the body is barbaric. Cultural differences aside, viewing has many benefits for survivors. (See pp. 10 and 16.)

- *Funerals are inconvenient.* Taking a few hours out of your week to demonstrate your love for the person who died and your support for survivors is not an inconvenience but a privilege.

- *Funerals and cremation are mutually exclusive.* A funeral (with or without the body present) may be held prior to cremation. Embalmed bodies are often cremated.

- *Funerals require the body to be embalmed.* Not necessarily. Depending on local regulations, funerals held shortly after the death may require no special means of preservation.

- *Funerals are only for religious people.* Not true. Non-religious ceremonies (which, by the way, need not be held in a church or officiated by a clergy person) can still meet the survivors' mourning needs as discussed in Part 2 of this booklet.

- *Funerals are rote and meaningless.* They needn't be. With forethought and planning, funerals can and should be personalized rituals reflecting the uniqueness of the bereaved family.

- *Funerals should reflect what the dead person wanted.* Not really . . . While pre-planning your funeral may help you reconcile yourself to your own mortality, funerals are primarily for the benefit of the living.

- *Funerals are only for grown-ups.* Anyone old enough to love is old enough to mourn. Children, too, have the right and the privilege to attend funerals. (See more on children and funerals, p. 54.)

hoped-for future reanimation, believers attempt to defy death. In fact, the motto of the Cryonics Society of New York is "Never say die."

These are some of the most prominent reasons for the current North American trend toward the deritualization of death. Give thought to what other influences may be impacting the deritualization of our culture and note them here.

_____

_____

_____

_____

_____

_____

_____

_____

_____

In her book *Brit-Think, America-Think* author Jane Walmsley summed up well the current North American mindset about death: "The single most important thing to know about Americans . . . is that they think death is optional." Unfortunately, today we do believe that mourning, if it is to be done at all, should be done quickly and privately—three days off work then back to the normal routine. No time for planning ceremonies. No need to drag out the pain. No use in dwelling on death. Should these messages continue to be internalized, we will see the continued deritualization of death in our culture.

"Primitive man faced his grief directly and worked out a system of personal and social rituals and symbols that made it possible for him to deal with it directly. Modern man does not seem to know how to proceed in the expression of this fundamental emotion. He has no generally accepted social patterns for dealing with death. His rituals are partial and unsatisfying. His funerals are apt to be meaningless and empty. Either he is so afraid of normal emotion that his funerals are sterile, or they are so steeped in superficialities that they remain meaningless, and the more normal emotions remain unengaged."

Reverend Edgar Jackson

Part 2:
Exploring the Purposes of
Meaningful Funeral Ceremonies

"When words are inadequate, have a ritual."
Anonymous

Rituals are symbolic activities that help us, together with our families and friends, express our deepest thoughts and feelings about life's most important events. Baptism celebrates the birth of a child and that child's acceptance into the church family. Birthday parties honor the passing of another year in the life of someone we love. Weddings publicly affirm the private love shared by two people.

What do such rituals have in common? First, they are typically public events. Families, friends, church members, villages, even nations—any group with strong emotional or philosophical ties—may create and enact a ritual, providing a support system for common beliefs and values. Rituals unite us.

Second, most rituals follow an established, cultural-specific procedure. American high school graduations, for example, begin with a procession of students in cap and gown, include one or more speeches and culminate when the graduates march across a platform to accept their diplomas. As with all rituals, the details will change somewhat from graduation to graduation, but the general pattern always remains recognizable. The predictability of ritual helps participants feel at ease. It also lends a sense of continuity, of the distillation of generations past, to those events we find most meaningful.

Spend a moment thinking about other rituals, religious or secular, past or present, that humankind has created to express that which it could not express otherwise. Consider, too, the rituals that have lent meaning to your life. Jot down a few notes here.

_____

_____

_____

_____

_____

_____

_____

_____

_____

Finally, and perhaps most important, rituals are symbolic. Wedding rings, christening gowns, mortar boards and gold watches all symbolize important life transitions and commitments. Not just the objects but the very acts of ritual are symbolic, as well. We blow out candles at birthday parties, for example, to symbolize the completion of another year. At a graduation ceremony's end, the graduates toss their caps into the air to symbolize their newfound freedom. What words could we possibly utter that would capture so well our feelings at these moments? The symbol of ritual provides us a means to express our beliefs and feelings when words alone will not do those beliefs and feelings justice.

The funeral ritual, too, is a public, traditional and symbolic means of expressing our beliefs, thoughts and feelings about the death of someone loved. Rich in history and rife with symbolism, the funeral ceremony helps us acknowledge the reality of the death, gives testimony to the life of the deceased, encourages the expression of grief in a way consistent with the culture's values, provides support to mourners, allows for the embracing of faith and beliefs about life and death, and offers continuity and hope for the living.

> *Rich in history and rife with symbolism, the funeral ceremony helps us acknowledge the reality of the death, gives testimony to the life of the deceased, encourages the expression of grief in a way consistent with the culture's values, provides support to mourners, allows for the embracing of faith and beliefs about life and death, and offers continuity and hope for the living.*

Now, let's look more specifically at the many purposes of the funeral. I have discovered that a helpful way to teach about the functions of authentic funeral ceremonies is to frame them up in the context of the "reconciliation needs of mourning"—my twist on what other author's have called the "tasks of mourning." The reconciliation needs of mourning are the six needs that I believe to be the most central to healing in grief. In other words, bereaved people who have these needs met, through their own grief work and through the love and compassion of those around them, are most often able to reconcile their grief and go on to find continued meaning in life and living.

Reconciliation versus resolution

In many grief models, the final dimension of bereavement is referred to as resolution. Other paradigms use the terms recovery, re-establishment or reorganization. The problem with this dimension as defined in these ways is that people do not "get over" grief.

Reconciliation is a term I find more appropriate for what occurs as the bereaved person works to integrate the new reality of moving forward in life without the physical presence of the person who died. With reconciliation comes a renewed sense of energy and confidence, an ability to fully acknowledge the reality of the death, and a capacity to become reinvolved in the activities of living.

As the experience of reconciliation unfolds, the mourner recognizes that life will be different without the presence of the person who died. The sharp, ever-present, pain of grief gives rise to a renewed sense of meaning and purpose. The feeling of loss does not completely disappear, yet softens, and the intense pangs of grief become less frequent. Hope for a continued life emerges.

14

As you read this section, please keep in mind that a meaningful ceremony is but one of many elements that influence a bereaved person's ability to have his or her grief needs met. Obviously, healing in grief is not an event but a process that will unfold for weeks, months and even years after the funeral itself. The funeral is a ritual of ending, but it only marks the beginning of the healing process. Even so, a meaningful funeral can certainly begin to meet all six reconciliation needs, setting the tone for the grief journey to come.

Here I would also like to introduce the concept of "dosing" grief. The bereaved cannot deal with their grief all at once; if they tried to, they would die. Instead, they must "dose" their grief by allowing in the pain and other strong emotions a bit at a time. The meaningful funeral allows mourners to get one of their first doses of grief and life as it now will be in the context of a social support system. To take the medicinal analogy of dosing one step further, the funeral provides us with a supportive atmosphere in which to take the initial pain of our grief much as our parents provided us with soothing words and loving caresses when as children we had to take our medicine.

The funeral is a ritual of ending, but it only marks the beginning of the healing process.

Before we move on, let's remind ourselves of the important distinction between the terms grief and mourning. Grief is the internal thoughts and feeling of loss and pain, whereas mourning is the outward, shared expression of that grief—or grief gone public. All bereaved families grieve when someone they love dies. But if they are to heal, they must have a safe, accepting atmosphere in which they can mourn. A meaningful funeral ritual can provide them with such an atmosphere for expression of their early grief.

How the authentic funeral helps meet the six reconciliation needs of mourning

Mourning Need #1. Acknowledge the reality of the death.

When someone loved dies, we must openly acknowledge the reality and the finality of the death if we are to move forward with our grief. Typically, we embrace this reality in two phases. First we acknowledge the death with our minds; we are told that someone we loved has died and, intellectually at least, we understand the fact of the death. Over the course of the following days and weeks, and with the gentle understanding of those around us, we begin to acknowledge the reality of the death in our hearts.

Meaningful funeral ceremonies can serve as wonderful points of departure for "head understanding" of the death. Intellectually, funerals teach us that someone we loved is now dead, even though up until the funeral we may have denied this fact. When we contact the funeral home, set a time for the service, plan the ceremony, view the body, perhaps even choose clothing and jewelry for the body, we cannot avoid acknowledging that the person has died. When we see the casket being lowered into the ground, we are witness to death's finality.

Though I have already touched on this point in this booklet's first section (see p. 10), here I would like to reemphasize the importance of open casket visitations and funeral services to the need to acknowledge the reality of the death. For mourners, to be invited to see the body is to be invited to say goodbye and to touch one last time that person they loved so much. It is also to be invited to confront our disbelief that someone we cared deeply about is gone and cannot return. Far from being morbid or carnivalesque, open casket services help us acknowledge the reality of the death and transition from life as it was to life as it is now.

Of course, we must respect cultural and religious differences concerning the treatment of and focus on the body.

"At the time when one should be joyous—be joyous. And when it is time to mourn—mourn."
Midrash: Genesis Rabai 27:7

When we contact the funeral home, set a time for the service, plan the ceremony, view the body, perhaps even choose clothing and jewelry for the body, we cannot avoid acknowledging that the person has died.

16

Judaism, for example, prohibits embalming or any cosmetic "restoration." Viewing of the body is seen as a violation of the rights of the dead. However, the general North American trend away from viewing the body is a trend to be concerned about.

Mourning Need #2. Move toward the pain of the loss.

As our acknowledgment of the death progresses from what I call "head understanding" to "heart understanding," we begin to embrace the pain of the loss—another need the bereaved must have met if they are to heal. Healthy grief means expressing our painful thoughts and feelings, and healthy funeral ceremonies allow us to do just that.

People tend to cry, even sob and wail, at funerals because funerals force us to concentrate on the fact of the death and our feelings, often excruciatingly painful, about that death. For at least an hour or two—longer for mourners who plan the ceremony or attend the visitation—those attending the funeral are not able to intellectualize or distance themselves from the pain of their grief. To their credit, funerals also provide us with an accepted venue for our painful feelings. They are perhaps the only time and place, in fact, during which we as a society condone such openly outward expression of our sadness.

Like no other time before or after the death, the funeral invites us to focus on our past relationship with that one, single person and to share those memories with others.

Mourning Need #3. Remember the person who died.

To heal in grief, we must shift our relationship with the person who died from one of physical presence to one of memory. The authentic funeral encourages us to begin this shift, for it provides a natural time and place for us to think about the moments we shared—good and bad—with the person who died. Like no other time before or after the death, the funeral invites us to focus on our past relationship with that one, single person and to share those memories with others.

At traditional funerals, the eulogy attempts to highlight

the major events in the life of the deceased and the characteristics that he or she most prominently displayed. This is helpful to mourners, for it tends to prompt more intimate, individualized memories. Later, after the ceremony itself, many mourners will informally share memories of the person who died. This, too, is meaningful. Throughout our grief journeys, the more we are able to "tell the story"—of the death itself, of our memories of the person who died—the more likely we will be to reconcile our grief. Moreover, the sharing of memories at the funeral affirms the worth we have placed on the person who died, legitimizing our pain. Often, too, the memories others choose to share with us at the funeral are memories that we have not heard before. This teaches us about the dead person's life apart from ours and allows us glimpses into that life that we may cherish forever.

Mourning Need #4. Develop a new self-identity.

Another primary reconciliation need of mourning is the development of a new self-identity. We are all social beings whose lives are given meaning in relation to the lives of those around us. I am not just Alan Wolfelt, but a son, a brother, a husband, a father, a friend. When someone close to me dies, my self-identity as defined in those ways changes.

Van Gennep, in his book *The Rites of Passage*, emphasized that funerals help mourners with their changed statuses. He pointed out that rites of birth, marriage and death mark separation from an old status, transition into a new status and incorporation into that new status. To use his term, funerals are a "rite of passage." In *The Ritual Process*, Turner reminded us that change in an individual's life is a potential threat to the whole social group, which knows how to treat someone in a clearly defined state but not someone who hovers between states.

The funeral helps us begin this difficult process of developing a new self-identity because it provides a social venue for public acknowledgment of our new roles. If you are a parent of a child and that child dies, the funeral marks the beginning of your life as a former parent (in the physical sense; you will always have that relationship through memory). Others attending the funeral are in effect saying, "We acknowledge your changed identity and we want you to know we still care about you." On the other hand, in situations where there is no funeral, the social group does not know how to relate to the person whose identity has

"We must listen to the music of the past to sing in the present and dance into the future."

Do funerals over-idealize the person who died?

Sometimes people feel uncomfortable when they attend the funeral of someone for whom they had mixed feelings: "Good father, loving husband, faithful friend—that's not the Joe I knew!" I have found that this funereal tendency to idealize the person who died helps mourners—primary mourners, especially—better cope with their initial feelings of loss and pain. So Joe wasn't always the greatest guy, but if you were his wife of 35 years, you don't need a rundown of his faults at the funeral. Instead, you need to feel that others loved Joe, too, and that they value your love for him.

Yes, funerals sometimes over-idealize the person who died. That's OK. Later on mourners can more privately contend with their ambivalent feelings.

changed and often that person is socially abandoned. In addition, having supportive friends and family around us at the time of the funeral helps us realize we literally still exist. This self-identity issue is illustrated by a comment the bereaved often make: "When he died, I felt like a part of me died, too."

Mourning Need #5. Search for meaning.

When someone loved dies, we naturally question the meaning of life and death. Why did this person die? Why now? Why this way? Why does it have to hurt so much? What happens after death? To heal in grief, we must explore these types of questions if we are to become reconciled to our grief. In fact, we must first ask these "why" questions to decide why we should go on living before we can ask ourselves how we will go on living. This does not mean we must find definitive answers, only that we need the opportunity to think (and feel) things through.

"When he died, I felt like a part of me died, too."

The funeral provides us with such an opportunity. For those who adhere to a specific religious faith, the meaningful funeral will reinforce that faith and provide comfort. Alternatively, it may prompt us to question our faith, which too can be an enriching process. Whether you agree or disagree with the belief system upheld by a particular funeral service may not matter; what may matter more is that you have held up your heart to that belief system and struggled with the gap.

On a more fundamental level, the funeral reinforces one central fact of our existence: we will die. Like living, dying is a natural and unavoidable process. (We North Americans tend not to acknowledge this.) Thus the funeral helps us search for meaning in the life and death of the person who died as well as in our own lives and impending deaths. Each funeral we attend serves as a sort of dress rehearsal for our own.

Funerals are a way in which we as individuals and as a community convey our beliefs and values about life and death. The very fact of a funeral demonstrates that death is important to us. For the living to go on living as fully and as healthily as possible, this is as it should be.

Mourning Need #6. Receive ongoing support from others.

As we have said, funerals are a public means of expressing our beliefs and feelings about the death of someone loved. In fact, funerals are the public venue for offering support to others and being supported in grief, both at the time of the funeral and into the future. Funerals make a social statement that says, "Come support me." Whether they realize it or not, those who choose not to have a funeral are saying, "Don't come support me."

Whether you agree or disagree with the belief system upheld by a particular funeral service may not matter; what may matter more is that you have held up your heart to that belief system and struggled with the gap.

People often attend funerals not for their own benefit (although they sometimes should examine this rationalization) but for the benefit of the primary mourners. An office worker's daughter is killed in a car accident, and although they didn't know the girl, the office worker's colleagues attend the funeral to demonstrate their support. The mother feels grateful and after her (skimpy) bereavement leave, returns to work hoping her grief will be acknowledged. This public affirmation value of funerals cannot be overemphasized.

Funerals let us physically demonstrate our support, too. Sadly, ours is not a demonstrative society, but at funerals we are "allowed" to embrace, to touch, to comfort. Again, words are inadequate so we nonverbally demonstrate our support. This physical show of support is one of the most important healing aspects of meaningful funeral ceremonies.

Funerals make a social statement that says, "Come support me." Whether they realize it or not, those who choose not to have a funeral are saying, "Don't come support me."

Another one is the helping relationships that are established at funerals. Friends often seek out ways in which they can help the primary mourners: May I bring the flowers

"The confrontation of death gives the most positive reality to life itself. It makes the individual's existence real, absolute and concrete. And my awareness of this gives my existence and what I do each hour an absolute quality."
Rollo May

"It's not that I mind death so much, it's just that I don't want to be there when it happens." Woody Allen

"Rituals build community, creating a meeting-ground where people can share deep feelings, positive and negative . . . a place where they can sing or scream, howl ecstatically or furiously, play, or keep a solemn silence."
Starhawk

back to the house? Would you like someone to watch little Susie for a few afternoons this week? I'd like to make a few meals for your family. When might be a good time to bring them over? Friends helping friends and strengthened relationships among the living are invaluable funeral offshoots.

Finally, and most simply, funerals serve as the central gathering place for mourners. When we care about someone who died or his family members, we attend the funeral if at all possible. Our physical presence is our most important show of support for the living. By attending the funeral we let everyone else there know that they are not alone in their grief.

Earlier I asked you to spend a few minutes brainstorming about both society's rituals past and present and the rituals you have found most important in your life. Now, while you're still thinking about the many beneficial purposes of the funeral, take a moment to jot down any additional purposes you can think of:

_____

_____

_____

_____

_____

_____

_____

_____

Summary—Purposes of the Meaningful Funeral

For quick review, I've gleaned the major purposes of the funeral discussed at length in this part of the booklet and listed them here.

Meaningful funerals . . .

. . . confirm that someone we loved has died.

. . . help us understand that death is final.

. . . allow us to say goodbye.

. . . serve as a private and public transition between our lives before the death to our lives after the death.

. . . encourage us to embrace and express our pain.

. . . help us remember the person who died and encourage us to share those memories with others.

. . . offer a time and place for us to talk about the life and death of the deceased.

. . . affirm the worth of our relationship with the person who died.

. . . provide a social support system for us and other mourners.

. . . help integrate mourners back into the community.

. . . allow us to search for meaning in life and death.

. . . reinforce the fact of death in all our lives.

. . . establish ongoing helping relationships among mourners.

Part 3:
The Caregiver's Role in Creating Meaningful Funeral Ceremonies

"The one who conducts the funeral . . . must have a capacity for empathy, understanding of the situation of mourners and knowing something of what they are feeling. He (or she) must be ready to accept the mourners as they are, not trying to press upon them attitudes or patterns of behavior that are not genuinely their own. . . Since no two situations are identical, there must be sufficient flexibility in the funeral to make it relevant and meaningful in each situation."

Paul Irion

What makes an effective funeral officiant? This is not a simple question to answer, for effective officiants have philosophies and "ways of being" as varied as those of the people they help.

Historically, funeral officiants have been clergy. Indeed, I expect that many of the caregivers who will read this booklet, particularly this section, are members of the clergy. To you I offer my professional thanks and respect for having for so many years upheld the tradition of the funeral; I hope the contents herein will challenge and renew your commitment to meaningfulness in the funeral ceremonies you officiate.

As society has become increasingly secular, however, a growing trend toward the use of laypeople—family members, friends of the family, funeral

---

Spend a few minutes thinking about the caregiver qualities you have found most helpful in your work with newly bereaved families. Think about your strengths as well as those of other funeral facilitators you know, then jot down your thoughts here:

_____

_____

_____

_____

_____

_____

_____

_____

When you've finished reading Part 3, come back to this box and see if you can brainstorm any additional helpful caregiver qualities.

directors, attorneys—as funeral facilitators has emerged. I welcome you, too, to this discussion. In fact, I believe that those families who come to the funeral process without religious ties are often better helped by secular officiants. Regardless of your background, if you are interested in helping the newly bereaved by planning and/or facilitating a funeral, I invite your consideration of this material.

You will note the use of the historical term funeral *officiant* as well as the more modern funeral *facilitator* throughout parts 3 & 4 of this booklet. The latter term may sound strange to traditionally-trained ears, but I use it purposely to invite new ways of thinking about funerals. To facilitate literally means "to make easier," and as I will discuss in this section, one of the most important roles of the funeral officiant is to ease and optimize the bereaved family's early grief. The word facilitator also implies openness and helpfulness, while officiant can smack of formality and hierarchical superiority—connotations that run counter to the model of funeral caregiving I support. Finally, a facilitator might be an uncle, a college buddy or an attorney, while an officiant is almost always a member of the clergy. To recognize both groups as funereal caregivers I use both terms.

Having said that defining an effective funeral facilitator is difficult, I must also say this: In my many years as a bereavement counselor and thanatologist, I have met some wonderful and some not so wonderful funeral facilitators and I have drawn some broadstroke conclusions about both groups. In this section I will explore the qualities that, based on my observations, effective funeral facilitators share.

The qualities of the effective funeral facilitator

Here's my list of effective funeral facilitator qualities, which I have designed to double as a self-assessment tool. As you read through it, I invite you to rate your skills in each area on a scale of 1 (low) to 5 (high). Be honest as you consider both your strengths and your weaknesses. For a more objective assessment, you might also have a friend or colleague rate your skills.

1. The willingness to adopt a "teach me" attitude.

Effective funeral facilitators are always learning from those they help. In fact, they realize that bereaved families are the only ones who can teach them about their unique experiences and needs. An effective funeral facilitator sits down with the newly bereaved family and, through a combination of listening and gentle guiding, in effect says, "Teach me what this death has been like for you. Teach me how I can best help you plan and carry out a meaningful funeral ceremony." This teach me attitude lets bereaved families know that above all else, you respect their thoughts and feelings.

What are the unique needs of this family? Is a traditional service appropriate for them? If not, what might be?

For experienced funeral facilitators, this means setting aside your preconceptions and your "standard" practices. Instead, I challenge you to view each new family in a special light. What are the unique needs of this family? Is a traditional service appropriate for them? If not, what might be? This "clean slate" approach can be draining and time-consuming, I admit, but rigid, cookie-cutter ceremonies are little better than no ceremony at all.

Low		Average		High
1	2	3	4	5

2. The desire and ability to connect with the bereaved family.

The effective funeral facilitator takes the time and expends the energy to connect to the newly bereaved family before the service. Too often I have witnessed the fast food approach to funeral planning: the funeral director makes the call to the funeral facilitator, often a clergy member, who then pencils in the time and date on his or her calendar. Little (sometimes none at all) contact is made with the bereaved family before the funeral. At the ceremony, the officiant pulls out his or her standard service, sprinkling the dead person's name and a few life details here and there. The bereaved family and friends leave the service as numb as when they arrived.

> *You must strive to understand the meaning of the family's experience instead of imposing meaning on that experience from the outside.*

Effective funerals are personalized (more about that in the last section of this booklet.) And effective funereal caregiving is personalized, too. You cannot help the newly bereaved family plan a meaningful funeral unless you are physically, emotionally and spiritually present for them in their time of need.

Low		Average		High
1	2	3	4	5

3. The capacity for empathy. Effective funeral facilitators are empathetic. This means you must develop the capacity to project yourself into the bereaved family's world and to be involved in the emotional suffering inherent in the work of grief. You must strive to understand the meaning of the family's experience instead of imposing meaning on that experience from the outside.

Listening, actively listening, is a critical part of empathy. Actually, listening is a critical component of all the qualities I have listed here. If you listen, the families you serve will tell you—through their words, their gestures, their presence—how you can best help them during this extraordinarily difficult time.

Low		Average		High
1	2	3	4	5

4. The capacity for warmth and caring. To be an effective funeral facilitator, you must strive for a sense of personal closeness, not professional distance, with the families you help. Though they will not often tell you this, they will be

"They sat with Job on the ground seven days and seven nights. No one spoke a word to him for they saw how very great he was suffering."
Job 3:13

"When somebody's presence does really make itself felt, it can refresh my inner being; it reveals me to myself, it makes me feel more fully myself than I should be if I were not exposed to its impact."
Gabriel Marcel

thinking, "Before I care about how much you know, I need to know about how much you care."

Warmth is primarily communicated nonverbally, through facial expressions, posture, gesture and touch. Yes, even touch. While you must assess each individual family's need for and openness to touch, you must also offer your touch when that need makes itself apparent. Remember, however, that touch is culture- and relationship-dependent and that before you can offer physical comfort, you must first establish a relationship with the bereaved family.

> "*B*efore I care about how much you know, I need to know about how much you care."

As a bereavement caregiver, you have an opportunity—a responsibility—to comfort grieving families and to be emotionally available to them.

Low		Average		High
1	2	3	4	5

5. An understanding of your professional and personal self.
Effective funeral facilitators understand that their past professional and private experiences with not just funerals but with grief in general affect their work. Actually, you bring the sum total of all your life's experiences to each family you help. You must strive to understand how your background, your strengths and weaknesses, your personal biases—your ways of being—color each funeral you facilitate.

Self-awareness is critical to the helping process. I truly believe that you cannot fully understand others unless you have first made the effort to fully understand yourself. Remind yourself each time you sit down with a newly bereaved family that your primary responsibility is to identify their needs and wants and then to help them carry out those needs and wants in the form of a meaningful funeral ceremony. Meaningful for *them*. They need your compassion and gentle guidance, not your insistence on a particular course of action.

Low		Average		High
1	2	3	4	5

"One of the startling discoveries of my life was when I noticed how trained I was to talk and how untrained I was to listen."
Pastor Doug Manning

"Comforting the mourner is an act of loving-kindness toward both the living and the dead."
Kitzur Shulkhan Arukh 193:11

Please Don't
Don'ts for funeral facilitators

Don't be a functionary. Be a facilitator. Think of creating funerals not as a chore but as your most important challenge.

Don't prescribe. Gently guide, instead. Avoid telling families what they must do or not do as part of their funeral.

Don't be rigid. Be flexible. Don't out-of-hand reject a special request just because it's "not been done before." Try to be flexible as you help each unique family.

Don't be defensive. Be understanding. The time immediately after a death is difficult for everyone involved. You are the figure most prominent during this time and as such can become a "whipping post" for the family's anger, fears and frustration. Try not to take it personally.

Don't forget about the family. Stay in touch. Bereaved families often complain to me that once the funeral is over, they never hear from the funeral officiant again. Families feel abandoned when this happens.

Don't under-commit. Spend some time with the family. Don't think you can create a meaningful funeral ceremony without first spending some time to get to know the family involved. You must create an alliance with the bereaved.

Don't over-commit. Know your limits. While you play a crucial role in helping families create meaningful funeral ceremonies, you can't be a super-person. Don't overextend yourself. Take the time to relax and reinvigorate. Ask for help.

6. The willingness to develop a personal theory of funeral facilitation. As a funeral facilitator, you believe your work is important. But it may have been years since you have been asked to articulate why.

Why do you believe funerals are important? What, specifically, constitutes a meaningful funeral ceremony? What do you see as your role in helping bereaved families with the funeral? These are the sorts of questions that, when answered, might go into your own personal philosophy of funerals. While we can borrow and build on the ideas of others, there is tremendous value in challenging ourselves to articulate our own key assumptions about the helping process.

Your personal funeral philosophy

Here are a few blank lines for you take notes about your personal funeral philosophy. I encourage you to later refine those notes into a formal, written statement that can guide you in your funeral work.

_____

_____

_____

_____

_____

_____

Low		Average		High
1	2	3	4	5

7.   The desire to seek new knowledge about grief and effective funeral facilitation. To continue to be effective, the bereavement caregiver must be committed to ongoing education. You must take advantage of new resources and training opportunities as they become available. The key, of course, is then to take your new insights and learn to apply them in your work with newly bereaved families.

Y ou must strive to understand how your background, your strengths and weaknesses, your personal biases—your ways of being—color each funeral you facilitate.

Experienced funeral facilitators also have an opportunity to educate others about the funeral ritual. Perhaps your colleagues would benefit from a regular roundtable discussion of their funeral work. Or surely your church or community group would be interested in a talk on some of the topics in this booklet. Challenge yourself to plan these types of knowledge-sharing. Of course, each time you meet a new bereaved family you have a responsibility to teach them about the importance of meaningful funeral rituals. This does not mean you must dictate what is best for them, but that you must provide them with the information they need to make sound decisions for themselves.

Low		Average		High
1	2	3	4	5

8. The capacity to feel personally adequate and to have self-respect. Helpful bereavement caregivers feel good about themselves. They feel good about their ability to relate to newly bereaved families. Their sense of self-value invites the same self-assuredness in the families they help.

*E*xperienced funeral facilitators also have an opportunity to educate others about the funeral ritual.

Effective funeral facilitators never feel superior to those they help, however. They offer their knowledge and experience freely, gladly. They do not talk down to bereaved families and they do not let their time constraints make the families feel they are being rushed or neglected.

Low		Average		High
1	2	3	4	5

9. The ability to recognize and accept one's personal power in the helping relationship. Tremendous responsibility comes with the helping relationship you have been entrusted with. Because support is so often lacking elsewhere, bereaved families will rely on you—sometimes you alone—to help them through their early weeks of grief. Do not be frightened by this temporary, heightened dependence on you.

But do not misuse this power, either, You should not feel superior to the families you work with but instead realize that your helping role is to empower them by encouraging their own autonomy and discovery of strengths. Paradoxically, keeping your own personal power under control stimulates the personal power of the bereaved family.

Low		Average		High
1	2	3	4	5

10. The desire for continued growth, both personally and professionally. Effective bereavement caregivers continually assess their strengths and weaknesses. They stay in touch with their own losses and how those losses influence and change their lives. In the same way that they encourage the families they work with to grow, they strive to clarify their own values and live by them rather than by the expectations of those around them. They yearn to continue to live and grow each day.

Low		Average		High
1	2	3	4	5

So, how did you do? While there is no acceptable or unacceptable overall "score", I suggest that you examine those areas for which you circled a 1, 2 or even a 3. This is not to say that to be considered good at what you do, you as a funeral facilitator must "score" high in all the above areas. Instead, I urge you to use this list as a personal and professional challenge. Ask yourself, first of all, if you agree that the qualities I have enumerated are useful to effective funeral facilitation. You might then set a specific course of action for improving your skills where they are weak.

After six months or a year has passed, rerate yourself to check for improvement. If you take this self-assessment seriously, you may find it will help you gain insight into your work with bereaved families, enriching your career and perhaps most important, heightening the profound, healing benefits of a meaningful funeral ceremony for the bereaved people in your care.

Helping the newly bereaved is one of the most draining tasks on earth. But as many of you know, it can offer unparalleled satisfaction.

Helping the newly bereaved is one of the most draining tasks on earth. But as many of you know, it can offer unparalleled satisfaction. It follows, then, that while becoming a better helper to the newly bereaved is hard work, it, too, is well worth the effort. I challenge you to challenge yourselves and to hone those qualities that make you a better caregiver.

The Funeral Facilitator's Most Important Tasks

1. Listening

As I have said, empathetic listening is the essential helping skill. When you take the time to listen to newly bereaved families, you are letting them know that you do not have all the answers and that you need to hear their thoughts and feelings if you are to help them plan a funeral that will be meaningful to them.

2. Understanding

To understand the bereaved means to be familiar with those thoughts, feelings and behaviors common to the experience of grief, especially in the first few days following a death. Beyond understanding is the task of communicating this understanding back to the bereaved in a helpful way. You must adopt a "teach me" attitude if you are to truly understand each bereaved family's needs.

3. Educating

While a "teach me" attitude is essential to bereavement caregivers, so is the ability to educate bereaved families about the experience of grief and the funeral's role in beginning to assuage that grief. Let bereaved families know that what they are feeling and thinking is normal. Help them understand the importance of the funeral. Guide them through the funeral process—something they may have little or no experience with.

4. Supporting

If you are to help bereaved families heal, you must help support them not just through the funeral, but through the healthy reconciliation of their grief—a process which may take years. Be available to them before, during and after the funeral. Connect them with other support systems in your community.

5. Advocating

At times the funeral facilitator may need to advocate for the bereaved family. For example, you may need to intervene when a well-intentioned but misinformed friend encourages the family not to have a funeral. You may also need to convince an employer that the family wage earners need more than a day or two off work following the death. More generally, advocating for the bereaved means providing a safe atmosphere in which bereaved people feel safe to express whatever they are thinking and feeling.

6. Encouraging

The family who comes to you for help with funeral planning may think their acute grief will never subside. While you should be realistic about the ongoing pain they will likely encounter, you must also offer them hope for healing. Let them know that these first days and weeks after the death are among the most difficult and that with time and the gentle understanding of those around them, they can and will learn to reconcile their grief and go on to find continued meaning in life and living.

7. Referring

Funeral facilitators cannot be and should not be a bereaved family's only helping resource. While you do have the responsibility to put forth the time and energy to create a meaningful funeral and to follow up with the family in the weeks and months after the funeral, you must also realize your own limitations and when necessary, refer the family to other community resources for extra help. You are responsible *to* families, not *for* them.

Part 4:
Practical Ideas for Creating Meaningful Funerals

"It is crucial to be aware of the spiritual crisis on our planet . . . The unprecedented speed of social change has produced a massive collapse of the traditional system of religious beliefs, symbols, meanings and values for millions on planet earth. Traditional authority-centered ways of handling existential anxiety and satisfying spiritual needs are no longer acceptable or meaningful to them. But they have not yet developed new, more creative ways."

Howard Clinebell

Funerals are most meaningful when they are personalized tributes to the unique life and relationships of the person who died.

This is not to say that standard funeral services should not be used. Indeed, we have already acknowledged that established rituals often comfort participants. Traditional religious funeral ceremonies, especially, can provide a sense of meaningful structure and continuity. Indeed, the importance—historically and presently—of faith in the funeral ritual cannot be understated. Over the course of human history, most funeral ceremonies have been products of humankind's religious beliefs. The funeral, perhaps like no other event, calls into question the very meaning of life and death. So, each faith group has naturally created a funeral ceremony reflecting its beliefs about life and death and providing answers to our most profound questions: Why are we put on this earth? Why must we die? Is there life after death? For these reasons, religious funerals can be the most meaningful—at least to believers.

Many of you reading this booklet are members of the clergy and as such have given your lives to the beliefs upheld by your faith's funeral ceremonies. I respect your traditional, sanctioned ceremonies and am not asking you to abandon them.

But I do believe that standard funeral services, no matter how spiritually resonant, do not fully meet the needs of the bereaved *unless the service also captures the uniqueness of the person who died.* I am asking you to think of the ceremonies set forth in your books of worship as foundations on which a truly meaningful funeral for a particular family can be constructed.

I have said that the funeral exists to help meet the grief needs of survivors; Part 2 of this booklet contains a rather detailed discussion of the ways in which the meaningful funeral does this. In this last section I will offer practical suggestions for funeral planning by revisiting the six reconciliation needs of mourning and the various ways in which these needs can be met by the typical components of a funeral ceremony.

Wait a minute, you might say, there is no such thing as a typical funeral ceremony! It's true that funeral rituals can differ radically from culture to culture and faith to faith. Roman Catholics use a relatively formal ceremony that includes a vigil, a funeral Mass and the committal. The funeral itself consists of prayers, Bible readings, a homily, the liturgy of the Eucharist, communion and the closing rite of commendation. Orthodox Jewish funerals are characterized by expediency and simplicity; ideally the dead person's body (which must not be "viewed") is washed, dressed in white and buried before nightfall or at least within 24 hours of death. And in traditional Hindu funeral services, the family carries the dead body to the cremation chamber and lights the fire.

Still, North American funeral ceremonies, even among various faiths and cultures, include many of the same elements. Often they begin with a **visitation**, which is a time for mourners to view the dead body. Anywhere from several days to several minutes after the visitation, the funeral service itself begins, typically consisting of the **opening, readings, music,** the **eulogy** and a **closing**. Often following the funeral service is a procession to the cemetery and a short **committal** service. The funeral typically ends with mourners **gathering** together to share a meal and talk.

These are the common funereal components for which I will offer practical "reconciliation" suggestions. If the faith or belief system to which you belong has different funeral elements, I encourage you to examine them, as well, in light of the discussion that follows.

Planning the ceremony

When you first meet with bereaved families to plan the funeral, an excellent open-ended question to ask is, "What have you seen or experienced at funeral ceremonies that you liked? What didn't you like?" This gives them a chance to articulate their personal tastes before you offer your recommendations.

As I have emphasized already, helping the family plan a meaningful funeral is one of your most important tasks as funeral facilitator. Not only will a thorough planning session (or sessions) ensure a well-thought-out funeral, it will also help the newly bereaved family begin to meet some of the six reconciliation needs of mourning.

Simply by meeting with you and telling you about the life and death of the person who died, for example, the family is acknowledging the reality of the death. Another important "grief moment" during the planning phase occurs when families visit the funeral home to choose a casket. In my experience, this is one of the biggest moments of reality confrontation for mourners. Picking out clothes for the dead person is another.

And remember that the average North American family plans a funeral only once every 20 years. They may be unaware of their choices and their very role in planning the ceremony. Educate them about the importance of meaningful funeral ceremonies while remaining sensitive to their unique needs.

As you read through the following practical funeral sugges-
tions, think about the creative ways in which you might help
families meet their six reconciliation needs of mourning. I've
left room for your entries next to mine.

You'll note that there is some overlapping among the six
needs and that any given moment in the ceremony, whether it
be during a reading or music or the eulogy, will often help
mourners meet more than one reconciliation need at a time.
I do not mean to imply that grief is a series of discrete
emotional, cognitive and spiritual tasks.

However, I do hope the pages that follow, in addition to
offering you some new suggestions for funeral planning, will
help you begin to place a heightened emphasis on meeting the
grief needs of mourners during the funerals you officiate.

Visitation

The visitation (also called the wake or calling hours) is an historically rooted practice that unfortunately is being used less and less today. While it is not an element of the funeral that you as a funeral facilitator may help "plan", you do have a responsibility to educate bereaved families about the benefits of visitation and suggest some of the following ways to make it more meaningful for them. When at all possible, I also encourage you to attend the visitation yourself, no matter how briefly. Your presence will be seen as a supportive gesture and a confirmation of the family's choice to have a visitation.

Mourning need	Ways to meet this need	Your ideas
1. Acknowledge the reality of the death.	Simply having a visitation does much to help survivors begin to meet this need. Encourage mourners, including children, to attend.	
2. Move toward the pain of the loss.	Again, seeing the dead body may be in and of itself one of the most therapeutically painful yet important moments for survivors. Help them expect this. You may want to accompany the family into the room for the initial viewing, then give them the personal space and privacy they need. They will often remember you were there with them at this time. Suggest to families that they spend some private time with the body prior to the public visitation.	
3. Remember the person who died.	Because of its relatively loose structure, the visitation often finds mourners talking in small groups about the person who died. The registration book is often the first thing families look over after the viewing; make it more meaningful by leaving a column for special memories: "I remember when Bob..." Music that reflects the life of the dead person may be played in the background. With the family's permission, suggest that people put something special to them in the casket alongside	

Mourning need	Ways to meet this need	Your ideas
3. Remember the person who died. (continued)	the body. Children especially find this meaningful and may want to color a picture just for this purpose. Mourners of any age may want to write a letter, seal it and place it in the casket. Talk to mourners about their memories in preparation for your eulogy. Suggest the family create a memory table on which they display objects that link them to the person who died. Memory boards, on which people pin up a favorite memory of the person who died, are also popular.	
4. Develop a new self-identity.	The visitation is an initial dose of self-identity change. Simply by attending, mourners are coming together in a social situation for the first time to support the primary mourners in their new roles.	
5. Search for meaning.	Encourage family members to spend some time with the body as they begin to think through their "meaning of life" questions. Use a "Comforting the Bereaved" liturgy containing prayers, memories and psalms at the close of the visitation. Your words can then be used as a prelude to the funeral ceremony the next day.	
6. Receive support from others.	Encourage families to place an obituary and/or funeral notice in the local newspaper, even when it is a paid announcement. The support they may receive in return is well worth it. Educate the family about the supportive messages conveyed by the sending of flowers and the bringing of food. Model support by attending the visitation yourself. Remember to sign the registration book, for you will play a major part in the family history surrounding the death.	

Opening

A funeral's opening typically articulates the purpose for the event: John Smith has died and we have gathered together to remember his life and mourn his death. Though it may not be longer than a few sentences, the opening is important because it clearly marks the beginning of the funeral service and sets the tone for what is to follow.

Mourning need	Ways to meet this need	Your ideas
1. Acknowledge the reality of the death.	Use the name of the person who died. Depending on the circumstances, you might also mention how he or she died: "Many of you are aware that Mary has been ill with cancer over the past two years." Avoid euphemisms such as "expired."	
2. Move toward the pain of the loss.	Acknowledge the mourners' pain in your opening statements: "Blessed are they that mourn, for they shall be comforted" is appropriate for many people of faith.	
3. Remember the person who died.	Pause for a moment before beginning the ceremony's next segment to allow for reflection.	
4. Develop a new self-identity.	Acknowledge the interrelatedness of all mourners in attendance: "Our unique relationships with John Smith and his family bring us here today . . . "	
5. Search for meaning.	Acknowledge the mourners' search for meaning in your opening statements. You might say, "Many of us are asking why this has happened. . . "	
6. Receive support from others.	As you open, ask people to pause for a few moments and introduce themselves to those around them. This helps build mutual support. Thank everyone for coming and acknowledge their important roles in helping each other heal: "As Hillel said, 'Do not separate yourself from community.'	

Using Symbols to Create a Meaningful Ceremony

As you work with bereaved families to plan authentic funeral ceremonies, help them understand and draw on the healing power of symbols.

In the funeral ritual, symbols such as the cross (for Christians; other faiths use other symbols), flowers and candles—and of course the dead person's body—provide points of focus for the bereaved. Because they represent such profound beliefs, they also tend to encourage the expression of painful thoughts and feelings. Furthermore, symbols such as these provide the comfort of tradition. Their continuity and timelessness ground mourners at a time when all seems chaotic.

Symbolic acts, too, often enrich the grief-healing benefits of funerals. When mourners light a candle during the ceremony, for example, they are provided with a physical means of expressing their grief. Planting a memorial tree can be an emotional, physical and spiritual release; this act also creates a "point of mourning" for years to come.

The AIDS quilt and the Vietnam memorial wall are two beautiful, effective mourning symbols for all Americans. What small-scale, personalized symbols or symbolic acts might you be able to help bereaved families create before, during and after the funeral?

Below I have noted a few symbols often used in the context of the funeral ceremony. What others—traditional or untraditional—can you add?

Candle flames—spirit; also life's continuation even after death.

Cross—faith

Cup—nourishment, abundance, faith

Flowers—support, love, beauty

Mourning clothes—need for support, sadness

Water—source of life

_____

_____

_____

_____

_____

_____

_____

Readings

Religious funeral ceremonies typically contain a number of standard readings from the faith's body of literature. Like secular ceremonies, they may also allow time for readings that in some way represent the person who died. I encourage personalized readings—not to the exclusion of the former but at least as a supplement.

Mourning need	*Ways to meet this need*	*Your ideas*
1. Acknowledge the reality of the death.	Consider readings that specifically mention that death has occurred. At the funeral we are in the midst of death and at least some of the readings should reflect this fact.	
2. Move toward the pain of the loss.	Choose at least one or two readings that in some way help mourners' embrace their pain. Avoid using *just* uplifting, "he's gone to a better place" readings. As Kahlil Gibran wrote, "Your pain is the breaking of the shell that encloses your understanding."	
3. Remember the person who died.	Help select readings that best capture the unique life and philosophies of the person who died. Don't hesitate to inject some appropriate humor: "Bill told me just last month that he wanted his epitaph to read, "I told you I was sick." Preface each of these personalized readings with a few words about the reading's place in the dead person's life: "Auden was Bill's favorite poet. This poem is from a book Bill gave to Sarah on their first wedding anniversary."	
4. Develop a new self-identity	Involve people in attendance at the funeral in the readings. Ask a friend, a coworker, a family member, etc. to read a pre-selected piece or passage. (Remember they may need to have others standing with them as a means of support. Or, they may need you to be prepared to complete the reading if they are unable to.) Some may not want to read; for them a reading or a memory placed in the bulletin may help them feel included.	

Mourning need	Ways to meet this need	Your ideas
5. Search for meaning	Appropriate readings are one of the most important funereal vehicles for the mourners' search for meaning. Religious and secular philosophical readings alike typically place the death in a larger context of meaning and thus offer comfort to mourners. Encourage family members to consider personalized readings: "John will now share with us a poem his mother wrote for him when he was just 5 years old." Remember, readers may need your help in practicing the reading aloud before the service. Help choose readings that reflect the individual family's context of meaning.	
6. Receive support from others.	In some support communities, it may be appropriate for you to encourage those attending the funeral to hold hands during the readings. Responsive readings can demonstrate group support. Leader: "The Lord is my shepherd; I shall not want." All: "He makes me lie down in green pastures and leads me beside still waters."	

Music

As in many circumstances, music at the funeral helps set the mood. It is one way that we let people know that their emotions, which music tends to draw forth, are welcome at the funeral. Music is also a universal, unifying medium that joins mourners and speaks for them when words are inadequate.

Mourning need	Ways to meet this need	Your ideas
1. Acknowledge the reality of the death.	Quiet reflection during musical interludes often stimulates acknowledgment of the reality of the death, particularly when the chosen piece was a known favorite of the person who died: "One of Janet's favorite hymns was 'Lift Up Your Hearts.' As we join together in song, we realize she would smile with us while we embrace our memories of this faith-filled person."	
2. Move toward the pain of the loss.	Don't avoid music that helps people embrace their sadness. Music is often very moving to the bereaved and can provide an effective interlude for funeral attendees to think about their loss and embrace their pain.	
3. Remember the person who died.	Encourage family members to choose music that best represents or was meaningful to the person who died: "Wasn't your dad always walking around singing 'Amazing Grace'? Would it be appropriate to include that hymn in the funeral? Print a few words in the program about each piece of music's meaning in the life of the dead person: "The song 'Imagine' was one of Rachel's favorite's because. . ." While music is being played, create an instant memory book by giving each participant a sheet of paper for jotting down a special memory of the person who died. Collect and bind the sheets at the end of the service. A grandchild might be asked to make the cover for the memory book.	
4. Develop a new self-identity.	While an instrumental piece of music is being played, ask mourners to consider	

Mourning need	Ways to meet this need	Your ideas
4. Develop a new self-identity. (continued)	their own unique relationships with the person who died and how their lives will now change.	
5. Search for meaning.	Though music is very individualistic and people often bring their own unique meanings to any given piece, certain pieces of music speak to a body of faith and often bring mourners meaning. For example, 'How Great Thou Art' is a typical Christian hymn that helps mourners relate their loss to a broader context of meaning. At a more secular service I helped create we used 'The Circle of Life' from *The Lion King* and 'In My Life' by the Beatles. Have primary mourners light a candle while music is being played.	
6. Receive support from others.	Provide a time when music is being played for mourners to stand up and greet and comfort those around them.	

Eulogy (remembrance or homily)

The eulogy acknowledges the unique life of the person who died and affirms the significance of that life for all who shared in it. Without a eulogy and/or other personalized means of acknowledging this particular life and death, the funeral becomes an empty, cookie-cutter formality.

Mourning need	*Ways to meet this need*	*Your ideas*
1. Acknowledge the reality of the death.	Frequently use the name of the person who died. Revisit the circumstances of the death.	
2. Move toward the pain of the loss.	Acknowledge the pain mourners are feeling. Let mourners know that even if their faith embodies an afterlife, it is still necessary for them to mourn: "It has been said, 'At a time when one should be joyous, be joyous. And when it is time to mourn, mourn.' As we reflect on Jorge's life we may have moments of joy, but we will also probably feel intense sadness." If you, too, are a mourner in this funeral, model your own grief.	
3. Remember the person who died.	Done well, the eulogy can be the most memory-filled moment in the funeral. Write a meaningful eulogy by incorporating memories from many different people. If you didn't know the person yourself, consider having someone else perform the eulogy. Plan a less formal eulogy in which funeral participants are encouraged to stand up and share their most special memory of the person who died. (This may be greeted with some initial silence, but once someone speaks, this practice can be very moving and powerful.)	
4. Develop a new self-identity	Speak directly to those whose self-identities will be most affected by the death: spouses or lovers, children, parents. Acknowledge their struggle to redefine themselves. Make an effort	

46

Mourning need	Ways to meet this need	Your ideas
4. Develop a new self-identity. (continued)	to include societally unacknowledged mourners, such as gay lovers, girlfriends/boyfriends, divorced spouses. These "forgotten mourners" are in particular need of inclusion in the funeral process.	
5. Search for meaning	Acknowledge the mourners' search for meaning. Speak to the meaning that the unique person who died brought to the lives of all he knew. Frame your comments about the meaning of this life and this death in the context of the individual family's belief system: "During the holidays Betty and her family would read the poem 'Crossing the Bar.' Let's all join together in reading this poem."	
6. Receive support from others.	Tell those in attendance that their presence at the service speaks to the bereaved family at a time when words are inadequate.	

"The body of the person loved is no longer alive, but the memories will live on forever. That part of your whole being that loves him or her is embraced when you allow yourself the privilege of remembering."

Alan Wolfelt

Closing

Like the funeral's opening, the closing may be just a few words. But they are important words because they will likely leave a lasting impression on those in attendance.

Mourning need	*Ways to meet this need*	*Your ideas*
1. Acknowledge the reality of the death.	Sum up for mourners: "In bringing this service to a close we are symbolically acknowledging the ending of a life." Again, use the name of the person who died in your remarks.	
2. Move toward the pain of the loss.	Encourage the bereaved to embrace their pain in the weeks and months to come.	
3. Remember the person who died.	In your closing remarks, encourage mourners to silently reflect on the life of the person who died as they drive to the cemetery. Acknowledge that although the service is coming to a close, our relationship of memory with the person who died will continue on: "As we close, let's remember the words of Katie Brown McGowin who said, 'Little by little, step by step, I learned that I didn't need to hang on to the death to remember the life. What a joyous discovery.'"	
4. Develop a new self-identity.	Acknowledge the mourner's struggle for a new identity: "As we face the future without Lee, we acknowledge that we are forever changed by his death."	
5. Search for meaning.	Balance the embracing of pain with hope-filled, encouraging words. Close with an uplifting reading or song: "Let's close with a reading titled 'Hope.' Please join me."	

Mourning need	Ways to meet this need	Your ideas
6. Receive support from others.	Encourage people to continue to support each other as they continue to journey through grief. Ask them to make a mental promise to phone or visit at least one other person in the room within the next week. Let participants know what the immediate needs of the primary mourners are: "Joanne is unable to drive her car, so she will be needing some help getting groceries and running other errands."	

Committal

The burial of the body not only helps us acknowledge the reality and the finality of death, it also symbolizes the separation that the death has created. For these and other reasons described below, I encourage families to have committal services when at all possible and appropriate.

Mourning need	Ways to meet this need	Your ideas
1. Acknowledge the reality of the death.	Create a service that includes the actual lowering of the casket into the ground. Have mourners throw handfuls of dirt into the gravesite. (Don't prescribe this but offer it to those who may find it meaningful.)	
2. Move toward the pain of the loss.	This may not be the most appropriate time during the ceremony for you to attempt to solicit the embracing of pain. Mourners will naturally confront their pain during the burial.	
3. Remember the person who died.	Select one brief, final reading that captures the life of the person who died. Observe a moment of silence in which each person thinks about their unique memories of the person who died: "Molly used to love to recite this Irish Blessing. You may remember her words as she smiled and said . . . "	
4. Develop a new self-identity.	This need is often self-apparent, particularly as mourners walk away from the body in the burial spot.	

Mourning need	Ways to meet this need	Your ideas
5. Search for meaning.	The committal is the funeral officiant's last opportunity to relate the death to a context of meaning. Because they are spoken last, your committal words may also be those that participants best remember: "As Don always said, 'Please remember me always for the love and the laughter.'" Read a spiritual passage, quotation or poem that helps put the death into perspective for the family: "As we close, I ask you to join me in the 'Prayer for Those Who Mourn' . . ."	
6. Receive support from others.	Verbally invite everyone to attend the gathering and emphasize the importance of ongoing support. You might also print the invitation at the bottom of the service program. Don't forget to include directions to the gathering's location.	

"Hope is not pretending that troubles don't exist . . .
It is the trust that they will not last forever,
That hurts will be healed and difficulties overcome . . .
It is faith that a source of strength and renewal
Lies within to lead us through the dark to the sunshine."

Anonymous

Gathering

Most funerals formally come to an end when the mourners gather to share a meal and to talk about the person who died. These gatherings often take place in a church meeting room, at a restaurant or at a home of a friend of family member. Like the visitation, the post-funeral gathering is an element of the funeral that facilitators don't often plan. Still, you might offer these suggestions to family members "in charge" of the gathering:

Mourning need	Ways to meet this need	Your ideas
1. Acknowledge the reality of the death.	The meaningful funeral will have fully dosed mourners with this reality by now. A natural "telling of the stories" of the person's life and death often take place, helping this need be met in doses.	
2. Move toward the pain of the loss.	Again, no conscious "pain-invoking" is necessary at this point. You might, however, educate the family about the importance of a gathering atmosphere that allows many different thoughts and feelings.	
3. Remember the person who died.	Designate a memory table on which friends and family members place items that capture the personality of the person who died and the unique relationships that person had. Photos, trophies, clothing and cherished belongings are all appropriate items for a memory table. (This may have already been done at the visitation.) The table then becomes a place for mourners to visit and have private thoughts. Some families are using this time to share a memory video of the person who died. This is where still photos (or possibly video footage) are edited together, often with music in the background, to create a montage of the person's life. Other families find a memory video too much work at this time, but may put one together and view it later on.	

Mourning need	Ways to meet this need	Your ideas
4. Develop a new self-identity.	By encouraging families to have a gathering you have helped them work on this mourning need.	
5. Search for meaning.	People will often talk in small groups at the gathering about their personal theories of life and death: "I figure that cancer is just one of God's ways of ending people's time on earth." Let the bereaved family know that this kind of discussion is valuable, but if other mourn ers are offering platitudes that seem unhelpful to them, they shouldn't take them to heart.	
6. Receive support from others.	The post-funeral gathering is a natural time for fellowship. At the gathering you might let the family know when you will be contacting them again.	

"Let us pray for ourselves, who are severely tested by death, that we do not try to minimize this loss or seek to escape from it, and also that we do not brood over it so that it overwhelms us and isolates us from others. May God grant us new courage and confidence to face life. Amen."

Including children in the funeral

Most of the rituals in our society focus on children. What would birthdays or Christmas be without kids? Unfortunately, the funeral ritual, whose purpose is to help bereaved people begin to heal, is for many adults not seen as a ritual for kids. Too often, children are not included in the funeral because adults want to protect them. The funeral is painful, they reason, so I will shelter the children from this pain. Yes, funerals can be very painful, but children have the same right and privilege to participate in them as adults do.

As a funeral facilitator, you can help appropriately include children by:

- **Helping parents explain the funeral to their children**

  Unless they have attended one before, children don't know what to expect from a funeral. You can help by explaining what will happen before, during and after the ceremony. Give as many specifics as the child seems interested in hearing. If the body will be viewed either at a visitation or at the funeral itself, let the child know this in advance. Explain what the casket and the body will look like. If the body is to be cremated, explain what cremation means and what will happen to the ashes. You can also help children understand why we have funerals. Children need to know that the funeral is a time of sadness because someone has died, a time to honor the person who died, a time to help comfort and support each other and a time to affirm that life goes on.

- **Finding age-appropriate ways for children to take part in the funeral**

  When appropriate, you might invite children to actually take part in the funeral. Bereaved children feel included when they can share a favorite memory or read a special poem as part of the funeral. More shy children can participate by lighting a candle or placing something special (a momento, a drawing, a letter or a photo, for example) in the casket. And many children feel more included when they are invited simply to help plan the funeral service.

- **Understanding and accepting the child's way of mourning**

  Help the family understand that children often need to accept their grief in doses, and that outward signs of grief may come and go. It is not unusual, for example, for children to want to roughhouse with their cousins during the visitation or play video games right after the funeral. Ask the parents to respect the child's need to be a child during this extraordinarily difficult time.

I have offered just a few suggestions for creating personalized, genuine funeral ceremonies. There are literally thousands of other ideas you might try as you help each individual family plan a funeral that will best meet their needs. Be creative and try not to be stifled by convention and formality. If your ideas help families meet the six reconciliation needs of mourning so that they can go on to find continued meaning in life and living—and in death— you will have done them a great service.

As gatekeepers of the death ritual, you are entrusted with a big responsibility. Helping people create meaningful funeral ceremonies, especially in this era of deritualization, is a daunting task. But it is also a critical one. I hope I have helped renew your commitment to every newly bereaved family in your care. Help them create meaningful funeral ceremonies and you will have helped society as a whole.

"Grief only becomes a tolerable and creative experience when love enables it to be shared with someone who really understands."
Simon Stephens

Authentic Funeral Ceremonies: An Outline

The following is provided as an outline for you to use as you design authentic funeral ceremonies. You may want to photocopy it each time you plan a funeral. Do not let this outline limit your creativity, however; it is intended only as a springboard for your own ideas. You will probably need more writing room than this form provides, so you may want to attach blank sheets of paper or write on the backs of your photocopied pages.

Remember that the funeral is for survivors, and that meaningful funeral rituals help mourners embark on healthy grief journeys. Keep the reconciliation needs of mourning and the ways in which those needs can partially be met during the funeral firmly in mind as you complete this outline:

Need #1: Acknowledge the reality of the death

Need #2: Move toward the pain of the loss

Need #3: Remember the person who died

Need #4: Develop a new self-identity

Need #5: Search for meaning

Need #6: Receive ongoing support from others

Name of the person who died: _____

Biographical information:

_____

_____

_____

_____

_____

_____

_____

_____

_____

_____

Survivors (list family, friends and other relationships you will want to acknowledge during the service):

_____

_____

_____

_____

_____

Planning the ceremony

Note what your general involvement or role in planning and facilitating this ceremony will be:

_____

_____

_____

_____

Need #1: Acknowledge the reality of the death

Need #2: Move toward the pain of the loss

Need #3: Remember the person who died

Need #4: Develop a new self-identity

Need #5: Search for meaning

Need #6: Receive ongoing support from others

Visitation

Date _____   Time _____   Location _____

Idea _____

_____ Mourning need(s) met_____

Idea _____

_____ Mourning need(s) met_____

The Ceremony

Date _____   Time _____   Location _____

The Opening

Idea _____

_____ Mourning need(s) met _____

Idea _____

_____ Mourning need(s) met _____

Readings

Idea _____

_____ Mourning need(s) met _____

Idea _____

_____ Mourning need(s) met _____

Need #1: Acknowledge the reality of the death

Need #2: Move toward the pain of the loss

Need #3: Remember the person who died

Need #4: Develop a new self-identity

Need #5: Search for meaning

Need #6: Receive ongoing support from others

Music

Idea _____

_____ Mourning need(s) met _____

Idea _____

_____ Mourning need(s) met _____

Eulogy

Idea _____

_____ Mourning need(s) met _____

Idea _____

_____ Mourning need(s) met _____

Closing

Idea _____

_____ Mourning need(s) met _____

Idea _____

_____ Mourning need(s) met _____

Committal

Idea _____

_____ Mourning need(s) met _____

Idea _____

_____ Mourning need(s) met _____

      Need #1: Acknowledge the reality of the death

      Need #2: Move toward the pain of the loss

      Need #3: Remember the person who died

      Need #4: Develop a new self-identity

      Need #5: Search for meaning

      Need #6: Receive ongoing support from others

Gathering

Idea _____

_____ Mourning need(s) met _____

Idea _____

_____ Mourning need(s) met _____

Special considerations

Here you may want to note the special considerations of this service. Are children among the primary mourners? How might they participate? Are there other mourners with special needs, e.g. a deaf person who might need someone to sign the service? Does the family want the service video- or audio-taped?

_____

_____

_____

_____

_____

_____

A Final Word

When someone we love dies, we must mourn if we are to fully love and live again. Yet, when the need to mourn is greatest, we seem most inclined to want to run away from it.

In this "mourning-avoiding" culture, more and more people appear to be running away from funerals. They are opting not to go through the doorway to their ultimate healing. As caregivers, we have both a responsibility and an opportunity to help our fellow human beings understand that to heal, they must mourn. And to mourn, they must have people around them who are understanding and supportive as they embrace the pain of their loss.

Meaningful funeral ceremonies provide us the forum to give testimony to the value we place on life. Funerals recognize that our love for someone has moved beyond the physical realm to the spiritual realm. What an opportunity and a privilege!

Yes, to experience and embrace the pain of loss is just as much a part of life as to experience the joy of love. The meaningful funeral ceremony provides a "safe place" were we can companion bereaved people as they fully enter into their grief.

We will be well-served to remember the powerful statement, "When words are inadequate, have a ritual." If we are able to "walk with" and be loving witnesses to people in their grief, chances are we can become a catalyst for a renewed sense of meaning and purpose in their continued lives.

Ten Freedoms for Creating Meaningful Funerals

(This list is written for bereaved families. Funeral facilitators may want to photocopy it and offer it as a handout as they work with families to plan the funeral.)

Meaningful funerals do not just happen. They are well-thought-out rituals that, at least for a day or two, demand your focus and your time. But the planning needn't be a burden if you keep in mind that the energy you expend now to create a personalized, inclusive ceremony will help you and other mourners in your grief journeys for years to come.

The following list is intended to empower you to create a funeral that will be meaningful to you and your family and friends. Remember—funerals are for the survivors.

1. You have the right to make use of ritual.

The funeral ritual does more than acknowledge the death of someone loved. It helps provide you with the support of caring people. It is a way for you and others who loved the person who died to say, "We mourn this death and we need each other during this painful time." If others tell you that rituals such as these are silly or unnecessary, don't listen.

2. You have the freedom to plan a funeral that will meet the unique needs of your family.

While you may find comfort and meaning in traditional funeral ceremonies, you also have the right to create a ceremony that reflects the unique personality of your family and the person who died. Do not be afraid to add personal touches to even traditional funerals.

3. You have the freedom to ask friends and family members to be involved in the funeral.

For many, funerals are most meaningful when they involve a variety of people who loved the person who died. You might ask others to give a reading, deliver the eulogy, play music or even help plan the funeral.

4. You have the freedom to view the body before and during the funeral.

While viewing the body is not appropriate for all cultures and faiths, many people find it helps them acknowledge the reality of the death. It also provides a way to say goodbye to the person who died. There are many benefits to viewings and open casket ceremonies; don't let others tell you this practice is morbid or wrong.

5. You have the freedom to embrace your pain during the funeral.

The funeral may be one of the most painful but also the most cathartic moments of your life. Allow yourself to embrace your pain and to express it openly. Do not be ashamed to cry. Find listeners who will accept your feelings no matter what they are.

6. You have the freedom to plan a funeral that will reflect your spirituality.

If faith is a part of your life, the funeral is an ideal time for you to uphold and find comfort in that faith. Those with more secular spiritual orientations also have the freedom to plan a ceremony that meets their needs.

7. You have the freedom to search for meaning before, during and after the funeral.

When someone loved dies, you may find yourself questioning your faith and the very meaning of life and death. This is natural and in no way wrong. Don't let others dismiss your search for meaning with clichéd responses such as, "It was God's will" or "Think of what you still have to be thankful for."

8. You have the freedom to make use of memory during the funeral.

Memories are one of the best legacies that exist after the death of someone loved. You will always remember. Ask your funeral officiant to include memories from many different people in the eulogy. Use a memory board or a memory table. Ask those attending the funeral to share with you their most special memory of the person who died.

9. You have the freedom to be tolerant of your physical and emotional limits.

Especially in the days immediately following the death, your feelings of loss and sadness will probably leave you feeling fatigued. Respect what your body and mind are telling you. Get daily rest. Eat balanced meals.

10. You have the freedom to move toward your grief and heal.

While the funeral is an event, your grief is not. Reconciling your grief will not happen quickly. Be patient and tolerant with yourself and avoid people who are impatient and intolerant with you, before, during and after the funeral. Neither you nor those around you must forget that the death of someone loved changes your life forever.

Recommended Readings

Following is a short list of readings that have informed and inspired me as, over the years, I have sought to understand the funeral ritual. I have also included two of my own books that include information on rituals and funereal caregiving.

Ceremonies for Change: Creating Personal Ritual to Heal Life's Hurts, Lynda S. Paladin, Stillpoint Publishing: Walpole, New Hampshire, 1991

Concerning Death: A Practical Guide for the Living, Earl A. Grollman, Beacon Press: Boston, 1974

Death and Grief: A Guide for Clergy, Alan D. Wolfelt, Accelerated Development: Muncie, IN, 1988

Death or Dust: What Happens to Dead Bodies?, Kenneth V. Iverson, M.D., Galen Press, Ltd.: Tucson, 1994

Final Celebrations: A Guide for Personal and Family Funeral Planning, Kathleen Sublette and Martin Flagg, Pathfinder Publishing of California: 1992

For the Bereaved: The Road to Recovery, Austin H. Kutscher et al, The Charles Press: Philadelphia 1990

The Funeral: Vestige or Value?, Paul E. Irion, Abingdon Press: Nashville, 1966

Grief, Dying and Death: Clinical Interventions for Caregivers, Theresa A. Rando, Research Press: Champaign, IL, 1984

A Manual and Guide for Those Who Conduct a Humanist Funeral Service, Paul Irion, Waverly Press: Baltimore, 1971

The Rites of Passage, A. Van Gennep, The University of Chicago Press: Chicago, 1960

Ritual and Pastoral Care, Elaine Ramshaw, Fortress Press: Philadelphia, 1987

Rituals for Living and Dying: From Life's Wounds to Spiritual Awakening, David Feinstein and Peg Elliott Mayo, Harper Collins: New York, 1990

Understanding Grief: Helping Yourself Heal, Alan D. Wolfelt, Accelerated Development: Muncie, IN, 1992

We Hope to Hear from You!

I would like to hear from you about the contents of *Creating Meaningful Funeral Ceremonies*. My writing plans include future revisions of this text and I would like to incorporate your comments—especially additional creative, practical ideas for the design of meaningful funeral ceremonies.

Please write to me at the following address:

Alan D. Wolfelt, Ph.D.
The Center for Loss and Life Transition
3735 Broken Bow Road
Fort Collins, CO 80526
(303) 226-6050
Fax (303) 226-6051

Sponsor or attend a workshop led by Dr. Wolfelt!

In addition to his writing and counseling, Dr. Wolfelt presents workshops across North America on bereavement-related topics—including creating meaningful funeral ceremonies. He also conducts seminars for bereavement caregivers at his Center for Loss and Life Transition in Fort Collins, Colorado. Please call or write him at the address to the left for more information.

About the author

Dr. Alan Wolfelt is a noted author, educator and practicing clinical thanatologist. Recipient of the Association for Death Education and Counseling's Death Educator Award, he serves as Director of the Center for Loss and Life Transition in Fort Collins, Colorado and is on the faculty at the University of Colorado Medical School in the Department of Family Medicine.

Dr. Wolfelt is known internationally for his outstanding work in the areas of adult and childhood grief. Among his other publications are the books *Understanding Grief: Helping Yourself Heal, Death and Grief: A Guide for Clergy* and *Healing the Bereaved Child: A Growth-Oriented Approach to Caregiving.*.